T0158895

NAKED ANGER

Bria Renee

authorHOUSE®

AuthorHouse™
1663 Liberty Drive
Bloomington, IN 47403
www.authorhouse.com
Phone: 833-262-8899

Published by AuthorHouse 03/30/2022

ISBN: 978-1-6655-5632-3 (sc)
ISBN: 978-1-6655-5631-6 (e)

Library of Congress Control Number: 2022906056

Print information available on the last page.

Any people depicted in stock imagery provided by Getty Images are models, and such images are being used for illustrative purposes only. Certain stock imagery © Getty Images.

This book is printed on acid-free paper.

Contents

Welcome to divine days

Souls danced with joy in the dark

don't you think it's pretty?

countless lights in the darkness

one little light can be enough to keep you from
fearing the dark or losing your way

Light represents hope

Am I your light?

There are so many options open

So many potentials and possibilities

no more heartbreak hotel

looking to explore

someone could sweep me off my feet

and treat me like a priority

but for now

training my brain to find new connections and opportunities

Surprised the poor couch didn't break on account of us

Fell on the floor out of drunken brokenness

"I needed you" I cried

woke up in his arms

Ate ice cream early in the afternoon

Both of us slept on the floor by the fan to
cool down from the intense heat

Being undervalued plummets your real worth

You're tired but you're not giving up

You need daily doses of calmness

Acknowledge the testament of knowing what to tolerate

Don't be afraid to rock alone

The sun be alone every day and still shine

Be addicted to bettering yourself

When you know your worth

No one can make you feel worthless

You're the photo in my bedroom I wet
kissed out of obsessed fandom

Trees danced outside of my windowsill
as the wind teases the leaves

Sunny Fridays are always a promising one

Basking in the sun while showing off the work
in progress of my once insecure body

Fantasize how would we meet

On a decades old sidewalk in a hustle and bustle city or in a
southern town while leaving out a town's infamous eatery

In the end you're my obsession because there are
million tiny things you never knew you were doing

Apologies are pointless to me

Relentless, aren't you?

Change your behavior

When you finally give in

Your confused

Catered me sexually

But will you check on me mentally?

Just needed a peace of mind

Right on time

Nine times out of ten I'm disputing the principle

Not the person

Laying on your arms cuddled up watching TV was the best

Fighting the urge to lick his chest while he's counting hogs

You got me where you want me

Don't regret the fussing

These times are bold

But a bit scary

Digging too many graves from massacres

Social agendas can be swayed wrongfully

Systematic racism is real and seen visually
and ignored to be corrected

Give comprehensive ideas to steer important
issues in America's faces and minds

Birth more economic equality and cease
inciting criminality towards minorities

Seeing my brother depart

"So soon" I thought

Gathering my thoughts while on the open road

Eager to make it on time

Mom cried out of being so proud

Off to start protecting this land called America

AKA the land of the free and the home of the brave

Come back home safe and sound my brother

Inspired us all to be great

Gifted a priceless friendship

But testing its longevity

Forged out of respect and honesty

Given both our spirits a much-needed lift

an ear to always listen

To correct each other and advise

Will a line be crossed?

if so, will it be different, or nothing changes?

Wish I could've chosen another person to make a life with

Why won't you believe me?

You're going by what you heard from others

Please get your own view of me because people tell lies

He's yours

Your own flesh and blood

Please pray for me

I want to be perfect like you

I etched an indelible mark into you

You'll be inside of me forever

the sweetness of your touch

A taste of your life

Surprised me with new positive experiences

Wishing that I graced you with my presence

Feeling your pulse always gets me in a daze

Blow my face with purple haze

His programming changed

He's trying

Really trying

Third eye is watching if he's really lying

The tone of your voice is arrogant

Confident

I can barely think straight around him

His comments always send butterflies
fluttering in my stomach

He looks at me with fire in his eyes

Waiting for permission

"I'm all yours" I said

He doesn't waste another second

His scent

His taste

His voice

and his body is driving me wild with desire

I'm unable to speak as the sensations blurred my thoughts

I feel safe in his embrace

I moan his name weakly

He kisses me everywhere until his hands find mine

He squeezes them gently as he enters me

Our hips are swaying in rhythm as he fills me up

He hits the sweet spot as he makes me lose all composure

We stayed cuddled up as we enjoyed the bliss we're floating in

Do I doubt everything he says?

Yes

Does he take accountability of his actions?

No

Does he check on me?

No

Little s**t does matter guys

Tell her she's beautiful every time you see her

Buy her some food even though she didn't ask

Ask about her day

Kiss her

Hug her

It all matters!

Something so small can make a woman happy

My fellow Gemini is worth seeing

and worth seeking for

He speaks my unknown language that's often
misinterpreted or misunderstood

It's been said my whole being illuminates like magic

Are you intimidated?

Just be vibrant as our sign

Kiss me digitally as I imagine enjoying
the Florida waters with you

I love you anger

You attack at signs of mistreatment and disrespect

It knows my treatment is to be treated as royalty

Cruel situations can kill away an individual's kindness

My version of anger has my kindness compromised

Extreme silence would come following slow breathing

That's it!

It's not worth losing

So I thank you anger for opening the realization to
fuel the bitterness of killing the cloud of doubt

I'm taking No(e)L's like the Grinch

In a pinch

Can I un-inch your five inches?

You must work it in

Call me Timmy Turner because it's fairly odd

Thought I was in awe

But was really blah

Back in my life

Felt like an act of God

Laying on your chest

Hot blooded

Toes curling

Rubbed my small hands on your crotch

Started swerving

Missed how you served your cock in two servings

A child doesn't have to be biologically yours
for you to love them like your own

It takes a strong man or woman to step up to the
plate and raise a child they didn't birth

Never replacing their biological mother and father

When first meeting someone, little did you know

Overtime you'll love them unconditionally

You'll develop closeness

Shared memories and laughter

Even investing their heart and soul into a child

Despite they may experience mistreatment and unfairness

The day will come when their acknowledged
for their wisdom and patience

For too they are a parent as well

Reading my vibe

Up and down

Feeling on your Brussel brush beard

It looks divine

Didn't mean to be so freaky

Toning it down

Knowing now how to approach you

With love and care

Couldn't help but to look at you

Your f***ing sexy

Wrapped your arms around me while we cuddle and rest

Many pecks on your lips and eyes glued to my heart

Smoking a blunt while holding me is
defined as his peacemaking

Handsome seed he has

Tormented by deep suffering

Feeling trapped in my own personal hell

I've walked the same danger trail and reacted differently

But have the same result

To understand my pain, swim the same
waters that drowned me

Be curious about my sadness and what makes me happy

Tears streaming down my cheeks

Shaking

Realizing how bad my heart was broken

Their living their lives

Not caring

Feel a pang of sadness at the thought

But quickly shake it off

God stripped them out of my life for a reason

Whatever I loss I know that I'll always get
something better in return and more

A wave of blues entices my sought-after mood

Tread carefully

It's peaceful but powerful

Its form can make you drown with the mixture of sadness

Either light or dark

It's coolness and rich essence brings back
centuries of eras that have been neglected

I hate you anger

Finding myself grumpy

debate on my psych eval

Pull back the attitude

The streets are mean

all the color from my face drained when confronted

A front is placed

To hide

The denial

Of lingering trauma

As I explained to mama

Burning tears that stings my cheek

I hate you anger

Don't take my edge away

Leave behind past terrors

We feel like children

With our feelings floating like gravity

It's never ending

Our hearts and smiles supposed to be their
profit to comprehend our whole being

Our souls are pure gold

Some can be cubic zirconium

Weeping over pain requires deep slow breaths

I hate to define this as a child-like feeling

Scary to admit that it's all too revealing

I must admit

He drilled joy and happiness into my spirit

Becoming a critic

As you listened to my expressions

No gimmicks

Do not prohibit my playful ways because of my age

I'm growing

Teach me as you guide your manly hands into my hair

As I stare

To learn

He deserves to be spoiled

Given that he feels like he's worthless

I like to find time to be in his space

to radiate hope and peace

Curlythickmess

Atone to the mess

The coils are rich

Thick and vicious

Smelling the moisture

Rinse by adding water like a plant

Nowhere finish styling

Marked as my birthright

Will never understand why they lay flat without a fight

Conform to natural

it's beautiful

Each strand has a heritage

Love its pride

Love its sass

Love its boldness

F**k n***a free

Pleasing myself between the sheets

Bandana wearing

Pant-less ass beauty

Called me

Scrumptious, am I?

Thighs and tits galore

Feed me more

To fuel my freakishly need to be adored

Swing the door shut

Don't they listen?

Make a decision

Having a feeling you rather be entangled with other women

Chocolate covered strawberries

Dripping from my lips

Give me tips

As I imagined being grabbed by my hips
Got a nice grip

Creative logic constantly undermined

Like I'm inhibited from being myself

How I define myself is in a constant state of transformation

Something always happens that makes
me question everything I believe

If I'm afraid of being myself

And started repressing myself

I may become a stranger to myself overtime

I feel alienated and alone

Like no one understands me

Knows who I'm really am

Having trouble handling my emotions

Coped by becoming sarcastic and passive-aggressive

Was my life ever balanced?

Was I able to rise from the ashes and turned into a Phoenix?

The hurt

Can you see me whispering a quiet plea?

Deceived too many times

Wanted to punch my hands until it turned red

Decorated their memories

"Why?" I thought

As a lesson learned

It was always a soap opera

"As the World Turns"

What am I to you?

Your "friend"?

Your "employee"?

Am I much more than that to you?

Never stop proving to me how important I 'am to you

Don't take it as a personal attack

Take it as an opportunity to repair or
strengthen the bond we're building

Nobody gets me

I 'am old but quite young

I'm goofy but also deep and complex

Romance is a challenge, but it does show that my
actions reveal why words don't hold no weight

My mind is developed and made huge
impacts in individuals' lives

In conclusion I'm odd but I'm an experience
that leaves behind good memories

Do you know our struggle?

Are you willing to address the root causes?

We cannot change your thoughts

We cannot change generation of hate

It is not an easy topic but listen generously to each other

We want to give you a view of how we faced injustice

Even if you don't see racial discrimination
as a national problem

Such a gentle matriarch

Understands each tragedy

Spreads his luminescence to others

Craves rebirth

Seen his legacy grown

Constantly digging new roots and tends to pluck rotten fruits

His eyes show deep emotion

They're disguised

But shines when he smiles with pride

Thrive to survive love's ruination

Often lived in a guilted cage

Forswear the sins I endured

There is no technique to surrender

To get past

Go through it

Freeing myself from outdated burdens

Ignorance is displayed

Tired of being played

Anger is pouring off me in waves

I hate this stage

Give me life like Pinocchio

Guide me of to know my rights and wrongs

Jiminy Cricket

To be specific

Break down my conscience psychologically

So far realizing a man gone be a man

Decreasing my sample of my worth to ignorant folks

Sniffing out your presence and now want you absent

Incorrect meaning of our confused affair

All I can do is stare but not say a word

Drunk with forgiveness but sober with my objective

Your alignment is on a swivel

Can we ever be civil?

You made it clear, but I doubt it was true

Built a wall

Never got completed

Know what to label us or just let it flow or leave me be

Sinful ways to have his way with me

I have feelings too

As he plays with me

Baby girl

This is a no-brainer

Draining his feelings like water in a strainer

Morning moans

Sniffing you like a flower

Pheromones

Cursing you for your hatred

Chicken bones

Watch your tone

I 'am grown

I can stand alone

Crying on your broad shoulder

I felt safe

Always been told to don't rush into things

Tried to wait but given a list of excuses

Character is revealed when pressure is applied

I'm a ready woman

In need of a ready man

I want a diamond representing preparation of marriage

Not a waste of years or months

Why wait years if you love me

What is the issue?

Are you not ready?

Do you even love me?

Baby steps are applied to relieve the pressure

I sympathize with the mother

Whose intentions are to fix what's broken

But the son needs to be the one to reach out and
fix the damage he brought down upon us

The biggest coward is the son who never was mature
enough to take care of his responsibility

And become a stable figure to us

A lot of dads break their daughters'
hearts before any dude did

That's what the son did

He broke my heart

I'm currently focusing on me

I'm not talking to anyone new

I'm not pursuing anyone new

I need to heal

I need to realize that being attracted to pain is not healthy

Standing on my self-worth is okay

Focus on your dreams

Nothing else

Become one with the healing sounds of the Tibetan bowls

Relax with the rain as it finds you peace

Let it rebalance your mind body and soul

Let your emotional energy respond to the bowls

Be calm and gain clarity

No stress

No worries

Tune into your body and just take deep breaths

Sleep tight and have a wonderful rest

You are strong.

You are beautiful.

I 'am worthy of receiving love.

I accept myself exactly as I 'am.

I 'am confident in making the right decisions.

I will take things one step at a time.

I 'am full of potential.

I survived this feeling before, and I can do it again.

Black music describes the dark catastrophe in one's life

The backdrop of the imagery is too painful to grasp

Many willing to cut against the grain

Some take time to blossom and to know their musical tenants

Calling to question the bigger question like Einstein

The stories are being told by experiences

And to speak their own futures into existence

Special thanks to my family and loved ones for pushing me to write these wonderful pieces and helping me to share my work to the world.

I wanted individuals who's able to read my pieces to learn and digest certain subject matters that is common among every community and to feel relatable about my personal experiences with not only life but with men as well.

I also wanted to thank Maryah_Art for designing my gorgeous book cover.

Printed in the United States
by Baker & Taylor Publisher Services